Poetry for Me

Poetry for Me

Noel Said Hassan

Dedication

I want to dedicate this book to my parents for supporting me in anything and everything I do. I want to thank my family for taking the time to fall in love with my poems and having faith in me throughout this whole process. I want to thank my favorite poets, Brother Tyson Amir and Ms. Ree Botts, for unlocking my inner poet and for being patient with me throughout my poetry journey. Without these amazing poets, I don't think I would've known that I was indeed, a poet. I also want to dedicate my book to all the Yemeni and Muslim kids who feel left out, and for all the young people who are trying to figure themselves out.

Table of Contents

Acknowledgements

Bismillah Al Rahman Al Rahim,

First I would like to thank my mother and best friend for showing me what a strong women is and for supporting me in every step of my poetry journey and in life. To my Baba, thank you for listening to me recite my poems and giving me support always in everything I do. To my grandparents **Ali** and **Zabibah**, thank you for teaching me to love being Yemeni and to be strong. To my **Geda Sagia** for listening to my poems and being my number one supporter always! To **Elias** for being my favorite brother! To **Maya** for being the cutest and happiest baby sister ever! Big thank you **Ms. Ree Botts** for inspiring me to join the Slam Club and for having a powerful voice that inspired me to write. Another special thank you to the city of **Oakland** and the **Youth Speaks Organization** for making an organization for people like me to explore poetry, my identity, my feelings, and my power as an Arab girl in America. Thank you to **Oakland Technical High School** for giving me the opportunity to learn and appreciate diversity, poetry and to fight for social change. An extra thank you to **Tyson Amir** for motivating, mentoring and guiding me through this whole process. To

Michelle Rostampour and **Lauren Markham**, I love you both for helping me edit my book and being strong inspiring women in my life.

A huge thank you to my family in Oakland and in Robbins for teaching that I can be a little bit of everything and still a whole lot of me: Aunt Jamellh, Uncle Hassen, Uncle Hussein, Uncle Ali, Uncle Ibrahim, Aunt Wardah, Uncle Saleh, Aunt Katie, Aunt Zaynab, Gad Mohsin, Uncle Ahmed, Aunt Sabah, Aunt Taheyah, Uncle Yaseen, Gad Mohsin and Gada Houida, Ameara, Amir, Amani, Inshirah, Aunt Dalal, Uncle Abdallah. Thank you for supporting me always in life. To all my cousins: Jamella, Sarah, Miriam, Selma, Noah, Adam, Zakaria, Sulaiman, Zayne, Hassan, Bessery, Gameel, Summer, Yusuf, Ali, Bilal, Mouad, Shayma, Adul Kareem, Mustafa, Sumaya, Amar, Ahmed, Taheyah, Anas, Gabriel and to all the other family members that I didn't name (because this list would go on forever) a huge thank you for all the love.

Introduction

In the last three years I found myself and found poetry that had been lost in my jumbled thoughts as a young teenager. Arab American, Yemeni Teen, and Muslim Girl are all the labels I have had to live with and navigate through to find my voice in poetry. I just wanted to find a place to share my feelings and thoughts, a place to be safe in my thoughts, heart and mind, and a way to release all that the world has placed on me. It felt like a burden to live with these feelings and this is how *Poetry for Me* came to life.

The journey started when I moved from a small country town in California back to Oakland, the city I'd been born in. I'd moved away in the third grade, and here I was coming back freshmen year of high school. I had a lot happening in my life: trying to understand my parents' divorce, dealing with being a teenager with new responsibilities and the move, and trying to control all my emotions; it all overwhelmed me. I made dua to Allah (swt) to help me with my weakness and to strengthen me in any hardships that were destined to come my way. My prayers were accepted. One day while I was at my new school, Oakland Technical High School, clubs were being held outside in the front of school. A lady, who I will later on get to know her as Ms. Ree, performed a poem of hers on the very front steps of the school. The emotion in her voice as she recited her poem, "She Can't Breathe," beckoned me to listen, and it awakened something hidden within me. I felt her power and the naked emotions she shared, and I longed to have these same abilities. To be free, to let all that lived within me flow out and awaken others. Before I knew it, I introduced myself to her, and she told me all the info I needed to join her club.

The Oakland Tech Slam Club wasn't an extracurricular activity to pad my college resume. It was an emotional need for my growth as a young woman. I couldn't wait to see my mom later that day at her school, to tell her about my new membership. She was just as excited as I was and couldn't wait for this new creative path to develop in me. The first couple of meetings, I realized quickly I was closed off, and I struggled to formulate my thoughts and at the same time, over thought every line I wrote. Too shy to share my poems, I didn't believe that I was good enough. I compared myself to others and even worse I didn't realize who I was.

Through trial and error and a lot of erasing and just writing, I found myself. I found the voice within me that I didn't know existed. My writing started to improve, then my form and style of writing started to finally fall into place. I overcame my fear of being vulnerable in front of an audience and found the power behind every single word in my poems. That's when I fell in love with poetry and wanted to take it to the next level. My mother, a teacher herself, saw how much I loved poetry and decided to introduce me to one of her favorite local poets and friend.

This is how I met my mentor, Brother Tyson Amir. He not only taught about poetry and the power it held but he also taught me the process of creating a book and even more importantly how to be patient with myself. He constantly stressed that the key to completing a masterpiece is to be organized. He opened my eyes through his book *Black Boys Poems* and showed me that I live in a world where unity and communication are power. But he validated my feelings and fears about the world around me. Living in a world where the KKK still exists and where the xenophobia and racism flourish openly. Sharing my poetry is important because the American Yemeni experience needs to be acknowledged. It needs a voice, and I found mine and am ready to share it. I am a 16-year-old with a story to tell, and it is as much a part of America as apple pie or aseed. I also want to share my poetry to inspire young people to write and to abandon fear and to be true to themselves. I want to be like Ms. Ree and help young people unlock their stories and feel compelled to release all emotions they have inside. I want the hairs on their arms to rise from hearing my passion and truth, forcing them to do the same.

Instructed on the Principles of Me

I didn't ask for your stares or for your
questioning looks
I didn't ask for you to look at me like I'm an alien
from outer space
We, breathing in the same air and standing in
the same place
I already told you that America is my birthplace
I didn't ask for your assumption, so just go away

I already told you that I don't date, in my
religious faith
Don't give me that pouting face, I don't need the
opposite sex to make me feel great
I only need the One and Only God who I call
Allah (swt), and he's protecting me from the
unnecessary crying and heartbreak
Besides, none of the guys that you throw at me
will ever meet the criteria anyway

When I walk down the halls, look into my
modesty and tell me what you think
Don't be scared, I won't blow up the school in
your face. I'm not a terrorist
I repeat, I am not a terrorist!
Calm down,
You're so petrified
You look like you're gonna faint

I'm just a teenage girl trying to accomplish her dreams. Like every normal ass kid in this world is trying to do

Why don't you see?

I didn't ask for a whole interview about Muslims and Islam when I am waiting in line to go to the bathroom
I just need to go pee.
Is that okay with you?
Or do I actually have to answer you because you've never seen a person like me before.
Wow, okay, let me pee first okay.
Let me urinate all of the answers to your questions so I can go rest in this ROOM.

I didn't ask for your entitled racist comments
We didn't do the terrorist acts.
We were praying to Allah when it all happened
We were in shock and awe like you
Just because we look similar from the outside doesn't mean we are the same within
We're not even close to the same
Maybe you should ask yourself that question?

Terrorist are heartless,
You know the ones who kill with drones
The ones who shoot first and ask later
The ones who choke the breath out of you
The ones who see brown skin and think criminal, different, other, illegal or feel fear.

Religious freedom is why my grandparents came

here
Muslims are peaceful,
Don't ever get us mixed up, do you hear!

Oh now I can't be angry
I thought I had a right to life and liberty
Now I have to give it up for your security
Trump temporarily banned Yemenis and other
Muslim countries
Wrap your bacon on my mosques' doors
Let's talk about this during a swine breakfast
Stop oppressing the Muslim brothers and sisters.

John Adams, your founding father said that the
"Prophet Muhammad (S) was a seeker of Truth".
Maybe you should read your own damn history
Or just read what your favorite daddies said.
Dysfunctional families and ignorant
communities

Please forgive me if I sound really harsh
But I'm done feeling torn apart
The Revolution inside me is bubbling, so I thank
God
No I thank Allah (swt) that "I was child-
instructed on the principles of freedom"

My Names

Noel is my English name
Which is ironically so
Because I don't celebrate Christmas
Which is the funniest thing of all.

Nowal is my real Arabic name
Which means I'm a gift full of kindness
Which has a deeper meaning than my English
name Noel.

But something about Noel is so simple
Light, easy to say
Easy for the non-foreign tongue to say
A solution for the English because they can't
pronounce my beautiful name
Nowal.

There is also a name for my adorable size
Mini.
Now, I don't disapprove of this nickname
because I am truly small from the outside
But tremendously strong and kind in the inside
My strength surprises because of my miniature
size
People stay shocked at the girl they see within
me
So please don't assume about people
Especially short people
Like me.

Now I have a shortcut to my English name which
is Noe.
I like this name because it has no meaning,
meaningless
A label that doesn't have any meaning is amazing
because it's not owned and dragged by a
definition of heavy words
A nickname that I've made cute and kind like the
person I am inside.

A nickname that is meaningless but seems to
have an abundance of meaning within the letters
A nickname that I have the power to give life to
A nickname that can be glued to my identity and
personality
A nickname that I am proud to own and to live
with

Names will cycle within the circle of life
And they will tell you their story
Of how they came to be
The most meaningful thing
That I've ever believed.

I Am a Woman Now

I am a woman now
Responsibility jumps at me
Body and Mind change dramatically
Thoughts are intensely differently

I am a woman now
Learning how to take care of my new body
Navigating the path I want to take
Understanding what it means to be a girl, female,
and a woman

I am a woman now
Need to help heave the weight of taking care of
my family
Being responsible for my actions
Being a good Muslim because now my sins are
being counted for
The urge of wanting to be good, so I can enter
Jannah.

I am a woman now
The attraction to boys my age is visibly in my
mind
But I keep it inside for my sake and to obey Allah
is so great
I need to show these boys why my religion states,
that "I Can't Date"

Because it wants to keep me safe, from suffering the trauma of heartbreak.

I am a woman now
Need to help Mama around the house
So she can finally get a break
So she can enjoy the advantages of having her baby girl
All grown.

I am a woman now
College is straight and marriage is around the corner
Marriage won't get in my way of achieving the goals that I've made
So marriage is going to have to wait.

I am a woman now
I want to support the young girls around me,
To help them follow their dreams, and be the girls that they are destined to be
I want them to see me as the wise sister whom they've never gotten for themselves
I want to pass down my knowledge to them and see them grow
Into the beautiful flowers that will grow through hardship and maturity.

I am a woman now
My beauty is shown brightest from the inside because my outer beauty is covered
So only good and respectful people will gravitate towards me.

My maturity is grand
My love will stand
My heart will expand, for those who see the
woman inside of me

I am a woman now.

Different

Being Different
Basically means
Being true to the person you are and who you
want to be.

Being Different
Basically means
Being a flower instead of a tree in the big forest
that everyone else wants to be.

Being Different
Basically means
Not following society's orders.

Being Different
Basically means
You are racially beautiful.

Being Different
Basically means
You are religiously faithful.

Being Different
Basically means
Loving every piece of yourself personally

Being Different

Basically means
Divergently unable to fit into a single category

Being Different
Basically means
Being brave and smart enough to walk away
from people who break your values

Being Different
Basically means
Dressing up in a non-fashionable way, so you
won't be the same as everyone else walking
around you all day

Being Different
Basically means
Being you
And that is the basic truth.

Mirror, Mirror on the Wall

Mirror, Mirror on the Wall.
Why do girls look at you for so long?
Is it to judge their body type?
To compare and contrast it to the human sticks
that walk around?
So that girls can be mesmerized by the
photoshopped pictures that magazines throw at
their faces?
Is it to get girls to fantasize what their body
would look like as a celebrity and how their fans
would just faint from their artificial and painted
beauty that they manage to deal with every day?

Mirror, Mirror on the Wall
Why do girls look at you for so long?
Is it to get girls to cover up their already
beautiful face with unnecessary paint that they
plaster all over the place?
Is it to put on those chemicals that "somehow
make them beautiful" even though they don't
belong there?
To cover up the pimples and zits that invade
their faces, even though they are signs that
shows that these girls have transformed into
women?
To cover up the battle scars that show their
strength, courage and endurance,
Scars that have an abundance of meaning and
for some reason these females want to cover that

up too!
Or is it to put that makeup on just because
everyone else is using it.
To feel accepted and to calm their insecurities
To put that makeup on to attract attention that
will only get them so far?

Mirror, Mirror on the Wall.
Why do girls look at you for so long?
Is it to find the pieces of cloth that will help them
fit in with everyone else?
Maybe it's to show off their money.
Or to show off that body to attract those people
they shouldn't want.

Mirror, Mirror on the Wall.
Why do girls look at you for so long?
Is it to see the reflection in front of them as you
see them criticize every centimeter of it?
Is it so you can point out their flaws that make
them human and not plastic dolls?
Is it so you make them question why God/Allah
(swt) gave them this imperfect body that keeps
you alive and moving?

Girls that look into this mirror for so long,
Throw it off that stupid wall!
Smash it! Break it!
Crush it into a million little pieces!
You never needed that mirror to tell you that
you're not beautiful.
You never need to be like everyone else, because
if you're like everyone else, then who will be you?
The original you. The unique you. The hot chick

who runs the halls you. The creative and kind you.
Be happy with who you are.
Allah (swt)/God made you beautiful even though you don't see it.
I see your beauty crystal clear and many others do too.
Please don't hurt yourself no more

Kill the mirror and your pain will be gone.

You don't need to follow society's norms of beauty. Be the beautiful rebel you are meant to be.

Mirror, Mirror on the Wall.
You will be forever gone.
From these young girls' souls
Once and for all.

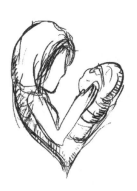

My Mama

My Mama.
The first daughter that my grandma had.
The first daughter in my family to go to college
and complete it thoroughly.
The first daughter to have my grandma's first
grandbaby.
Me.

My Mama.
The first person I saw
The first word I said
The first person to love me after Allah (swt)
The first person to help me find my way with the
guidance of Allah (swt) beside her.

My Mama.
The first woman to be my hero before I knew
who Khadijah (ra) was.
My mom, the source that helped me empower
myself
The first woman to love my flaws and to
understand the deep feelings inside of me.

My Mama.
The girl who struggled being one of the few
Muslims in her high school.
The girl who never gave up her one dream of

helping the people around her.
To educate and spread the love to people around her.
To complete her density of being the person she is meant to be.

My Mama
The lady who knows her strengths but also her weaknesses
She knows when to drop a bomb of knowledge or stay quiet
She knows when to make her voice loud and clear for everyone else to hear
The lady who surrounds herself with people who are worthy of having her by their side
The lady who didn't let others use her or pin her down
The lady who understands the difference between right and wrong with clarity.

My Mama.
Who knows me inside and out by using her psychic powers.
Who can read my thoughts like a mind reader
Who can see my feelings like a super hero with x-ray vision.

My Mama.
Who isn't just my mom, but also my best friend who I can lean on
The only person that will ever really know me truly
The person I can trust completely and will always give me her total honesty.

My Mama.
The one who believes in me and supports me in
everything I do.
The one who held me in her womb.
The one who cares for me tenderly.
So I can give back to her one day.

My Mama.
A mother who has Jannah under her feet
A mother of whom the Prophet Muhammad (S)
said, give your good company and love to your
"Mother three times more than your Father."
A mother who is blessed to have Allah (swt) in
her life

My Mama.
Who I love from the moon and back.
Who I love with all my heart
I am blessed to have her in my life
I can never thank Allah (swt) enough
For my beautiful mama

My Mama

Remember Me

Remember me.
As the little girl who has swum with the school of
Oakland Tech Kids.
The girl, who found herself deep inside this coral
reef called Oakland.
The girl, who wandered the opposite way of the
ocean current to find opportunities waiting for
her.
The girl, who didn't find following other fish in
her school tempting.
What she found tempting, was understanding
the huge ocean around her and making friends
who would help her understand it.

Remember me.
As the little girl that found her strengths and
learned how to appreciate her weaknesses.
She knows her limitations.
She understands that rules are meant to keep her
safe, but knows when these rules are meant to be
broken.

Remember me.
As the little girl who has felt sadness and pain,
and how her friends and family help her get
through the storm.
Her Friends.

My friends are the type of fish that radiates
kindness and trusts in their scales.
Who have brought out the best in me as I have
done for them
My friends, so diverse in character, that you'll
never find anyone like them.
My Family.
My family shines with love in their hearts and
understanding in their minds.
My family is one of a kind.
A species that carries honesty, love, confidence,
and determination in their bodies, in their souls,
and in their minds.

Remember me.
As the Muslim girl that has shared her religion
with you.
Who had shared her Yemeni culture with you.
Who has shared her kindness with you.
Who has shared her silliness and laughter with
you.
Who has shared her wisdom and intelligence
with you.

Remember me.
Because she is leaving this amazing coral reef to
embark on a new journey.
To a different ocean, to a different sea.
With different fish and different coral reefs.
A place so different from this beach.
That's where I'll be.
Remember me.

The Poetess and the Poet

A Poetess taught me to write
A Poet taught me to perform
They both taught me to open up
And to let my creativity soar

The Poetess taught me to be myself
She knew I was very shy
But she also knew there were stories and feelings
inside
She knew I needed time
To expose the things that I've kept in that needed
be let outside

I let loose the feelings like wild animals being set
free from their cages
You can say my stories and memories wrote their
way out of me
I couldn't believe what I wrote out on those very
sheets of lined paper
Those feelings and stories were supposed to be
locked up for later
When I was older enough to understand them
thoroughly
But I guess they began to feel the need to explode
I ignored them for too long
The timer decided to go off

The Poetess guided me through the writing
process

Rhyme, Rhythm, and Free Verse
Simile, Stanza, and Refrain
Personification, Figurative Language, and
Metaphor
Transformed into a style that seems right to me

The Poetess showed me the strength of being a
colored teenage girl.
She revealed to me the power of meditation and
how blissful it is to have a clear mind, relaxed
body, and soulful eyes.
The Poetess has taught me well
And my memories with her will always burn in
my mind

The Poet taught me to believe
He knew I was doubtful and unsure
About my writing skills and my voice
He saw past my shaky voice and my uneven
rhymes
He knew all I needed was practice, practice, and
more practice
He knew I had it inside

The Poet told me to stand tall in what I believe
Even though I thought I was small
Small in the sense that my voice wouldn't carry
the full load of meaning that my words are trying
to spread

The Poet appreciates my creativity and supports
me in everything that I do
He seems to be the only poet that sticks around
The Poetess left me to follow her dreams and to

inspire young people like me
I'm not mad at her, but I wish she could've
stayed
The Poet understands me deeply and personally
He is like the older brother that I never had
Well, actually he is my brother in Islam
And that is perfectly close enough to family
Wish I can see him more often too
But I am on the other side of world
While he is the City of Oakland
My birthplace, my home
That's where we've been together all along

The Poet prepared me to fight against the evil
The evils of this world such as racism, Shaitan,
and injustice
He wants me to fight for those who can't fight for
themselves
And I will fight
Not with violence though
But with my words, because words are never
forgotten, and they just as strong as the all-
powerful machine gun.
My words will be louder than the bullets
And they will ring in your ear like the effect of
having a bomb explode near

Both the Poet and the Poetess taught me to find
the meaning behind words
Both have taught me to be brave and to be strong
Both have taught me the patience of being an
artist
Both have taught me life lessons that will save
me in this life

Both have taught me to conquer my fears and to
try new things

And they both willingly let me be a part of their
lives
And I will be grateful of that till the day I die

Thanks to the Poet and Poetess
Because for every poem I write
Wouldn't be possible with you

Lions and Wolves

My mother's family are majestic Wolves
While my father's family are royal Lions
You can already see the enormous gap between
them
Wolves and Lions under the peace treaty of Allah
(swt)
But even then things still get torn apart
My mom and dad fell in love on their wedding
day
She the intelligent and beautiful Alpha daughter,
while my Baba the young and strong Prince of
the pride

Things didn't go as planned
They made me and my brother
Me and my brother are a special kind of species
Wolf mixed with Lion
Wolfion is what were called
A mix so special and so rare
That we are delivered and shared
Between lions and wolves so we can be with our
parents
Can you compare?

Traveling to the loud pridelands and back into
the quiet forest
We seem to adjust to every environment

It seems almost normal
But the memory will still stay the same
The roars and the howls of that night
When Mama and Baba got into a fight
But I was too scared, small, and young to
understand the roars, barks, howls, whimpers,
and hisses
I was too scared to walk out of my den to get a
drink of water for my parched throat because
that's what initially woke me
But those noises told me to wake up
I was so blind for not seeing the signs
I thought we would be fine and everything would
go back to normal
But that was such a comforting lie

You can say it all started when we moved out of
the pridelands.
Mama was born in the forest and she moved into
the pridelands to live with my Baba
But then Mama said she wanted us to move into
the forest to be closer with her family
So me and my brother can have a peaceful
childhood
Baba agreed to it and so did Geda Lioness
And so we moved
And that's when things began to change
drastically
Mama and Baba ran hours from the forest to
pridelands to hunt,
To make a living
Mama was fine with it
She seems to adjust to this move easily
But Baba wasn't having fun

He always came home late
Too tired from all the hunting and running
He looked like he wanted to give up
I stayed up late waiting for him to come home
Because that was something that I always looked
forward to
And when I heard him panting from outside
from his travels
I ran as fast as the cheetah
And he would enter the den with weariness on
his face
But when he saw me, he mustered all his energy
to smile and greet me with enthusiasm

Mama was off during the weekends but Baba
hunted six days a week and one day off
It seemed like we hardly spent any time at all
Mama seemed off and annoyed and Baba's
patience and creativity grew small
Watching the lions wrestle seemed to be his
entertainment of the day
I actually liked watching it too, but after a while
it seemed like we had nothing better to do
besides watch humans on screens and that was
fun, but like lions wrestling it also got too old
Before the move, we went on trips and explored
We would try new places and new foods and see
new faces
And sometimes we revisited some places
And created new memories and revealed old
ones too
But when we moved into the forest, nothing
seemed to ever move
And that's when I knew

Things were going to change real soon

The next day after the fight, me, my brother, and
Mama took flight
She said it was time for a change
And I believed her that day
When she said we wouldn't stay away for long
Well, that was my big mistake
To give myself hope we would stay.
I realized hope doesn't seem to like to stay
At least not for me anyway

Luckily we only moved one block away, we lived
with Ged Alpha and the Geda Alpha
While Baba stayed inside the place I once called
home
And we would visit him twice a week
Which seemed fine with me
That's when Baba began to change
He would take us out more often
His old self slowly started to come back
Something inside of him seem to uplift
Every time he saw us come into his home
My used to be home

But a strange thing began to happen
He would give me some of his game that he
caught during that week
And I knew this strange offering would be
permanent
When he gave that face of seriousness and
reassurance
The message was clear
Give the game to Mama

And you better not lose it

Time passed by, and Baba decided to move back
to the Pridelands
I honestly felt numb but knew that there was
nothing I could do
The pridelands are his home and the forest is
hers
I still haven't quite found mine
Or maybe I have but it's divided
Divided
That exactly how I felt and still feel
The feeling is now just a part of me
And I've learned to live with it
Deep within me

Word got around, the wolves stayed quiet in
respect while the lions started asking questions
which I gave them half-truth answers to.
Half-truth answers because they didn't deserve
my true answers and feelings
And partially because I was still trying to
understand what exactly was happening and how
I was feeling myself

Of course there is more to this story that I can't
tell because I am still trying to figure it out. All of
this happened when I was 11 so I wouldn't know
the whole story. Also I don't think I want to
know the whole story. I'll wait till either my lion
Baba or wolf Mama are ready to tell me. They'll
know when I'm ready

But one thing is left for certain

Sometimes things never go as planned
Especially in the world
Of Wolves and Lions

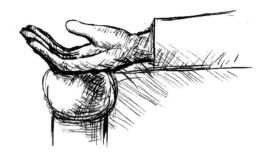

My Grandfather's Hands

My grandfather's hands are brown with white
spots, a skin condition he had since birth.
His hands, wrinkling from old age but full of
strength
His hands, worn from all the work he has done
for years, but they manage to keep going
His hands have survived many years of farming
and building
His hands transformed themselves into the tools
he needed to keep my family alive and well
His powerful hands have taught me that you can
be strong if you believe in yourself

His fingers have pointed out to me the path of
success and knowledge and I am blessed for his
wisdom and endurance
His fingers have dug deep into hardships and
now have turned white with content
His skin colors don't mix and they will never
change
He will always be the same person as he was
before the change of age

The lines of his hands map his escape of a war-
torn country to the land of milk and honey
His hands the shade of brown, worked the earth
of the valleys of Sacramento, Los Angeles, and

Fresno
His hands, mapping the years of traveling the
circuit as an immigrant searching for the
American Dream
The American Dream to live peacefully and to
raise his family faithfully and righteously
My grandfather, a United Farm Worker, Muslim,
Yemeni, and Farmer

My grandfather's hands have dug deep into the
earth to plant the seeds of strength and resilience
And he watched them grow
And he watched me grow too
And when I was old enough, I picked the fruit
from the grown plant of strength and picked a
flower from the grown plant of resilience

He watched me from the window and his smile
and eyes seem to brighten with pride
And watched me take a bite of the fruit of
strength and the power of strength grew within
me from that single bite
And I placed the flower of resilience in my hijab,
and it sent a surge of light within me
And that's when I knew
The importance of my grandfather's hands
Are deep within my roots too.

Split in Two

I am split in two
Am I a child or an adult?
Am I a city girl or a country girl?
Am I Noel or Nowal?
I don't have a clue.

I am split in two
Live in two homes
Mom and Dad don't get along
They are both from two different worlds
That I travel back and forth from.

I am split in two
I am mixed in with two different family histories
That all seem to connect and vary in such variety
But I'm the knot that keeps everyone together
So these family histories stay in their place.

I am split in two
Yemeni-American, American Yemeni
Do I actually have to choose?

I am split in two
Daddy's little girl in my Baba's eyes
Mommy's little woman in my Mama's eyes.

I am split in two
girl, Woman, Woman, girl
Which am I?

I am split in two
Jumping from house to house
School to School
Place to Place
Where do I belong in this huge outer space?

I am split in two
Seeing tear streaks on my friends' faces
Breaks my heart in two
I try to comfort them, but there is nothing else I
can really do

I am split in two
Thoughts bouncing in and out of my head
Creating feeling of distress
Lost in the list of my thoughts
Where was the ending to my list again?
I can't even recall

I am split in two
I won't pick a side
I'll never chose
I will find hope
And pray that it'll be all over soon

I am split in two
Till the end of this crazy ride of life
I will keep seeking the balance that I crave in this
life

I am split in two

My Journey with Poetry

My mother introduce me to Poetry
She said Hello and I said Hi
Me and Poetry met when I was five
Through Dr. Seuss and Shel Silverstein
I guess I am ashamed to say
After many years in being in my young childhood life
I didn't think of her much, after that day

My mother was my English teacher
In fifth grade, she made us write and read poetry
Every single day of the month of May
But when I wrote, I wasn't honest to Poetry, but I didn't lie to her either
I didn't open up to her right away
I was cautious that maybe she'll make fun of me
For all the emotional vibes within me
I just barely scratched the surface of my thoughts before I'd send them her way
Like a text message that wasn't really meant for her
Poetry knew that I was shy and that was truly not a lie

Freshmen year, I heard a woman pour her heart out in front of my school's steps
Where she stood tall and powerful with her voice

so strong and full of emotion
I couldn't believe the students around me were
not even paying no attention to her
Like she was a street singer in front of the
subway station in New York, where New Yorkers
ignored her completely like in Jack Agüeros's
poem "Sonnet for Heaven Below."
I was hypnotized by her voice and felt every word
come out of her bright, red lips.
Poetry was always there, and I didn't even realize
it until that exact moment
Poetry slid her hand into mine, and we both
listened to the beautiful women pour her soul
out to an audience that wasn't even listening
except me and Poetry

Later on, I am lucky to say, I discovered
That the same woman was actually the leader of
the poetry club which I just joined that exact
same day
I was so excited to meet such a woman

Meeting her was the real beginning of my
friendship and journey with Poetry
She guided me to understand that Poetry is a
friend that I can trust wholeheartedly
A friend that will always listen to you and never
judge you
Poetry will stay by your side through the good
and through the bad times

The leader of the poetry club was Ms. Ree
And she helped me believe in Poetry

And how powerful it is to have her by your side

Hand in Hand,
Poetry and I
Will stay together
Till the end of time

My Baba

My Baba
The funniest and coolest man I know
Who can crack you up with his jokes
And can rock his Warrior outfit in his little
Nissan

My Baba
Who can teach you how to dance to the beat
Or he can take you to all the sweet spots in the
Bay
He can make friends so easily; they rock with
him so calmly

My Baba
Making his own path
Without letting his past faze him

My Baba
Who's all about that relaxed life
And being stress free
His thoughts don't consume him
Which makes him a human being at peace

My Baba
Who'll listen to your weird stories
And he'll tell you his
He speaks his mind

But sometime he has a hard time
On deciding on where he wants to go out after
lunchtime

My Baba
Who likes to travel
And loves to explore

My Baba
He is the strong person with a stubborn mind
But that mind gets him by
And his respect for others, has gotten steer clear
of lies

My Baba
Who loves me most
But I will forever love him so such more.

The Death of My Cats

Hamlet got hit by a car
I was at daycare
Only four years old
Didn't know what death was
So all I said was bye

Jedi was a bad boy
He was playing with the wrong cats
He fought like a lion
His last fight had him limping home
Got there and collapsed on the floor
I was in San Diego having a great time
He was young and I said to him when he was
under the earth "I wish you had more time to live
a cat life, but instead you decided to pick fights.
Now look at you. My baby under the earth and I
didn't even have enough time to truly love you."

Mini was my friend from the start, since I was
five. She died when I was fourteen. She was my
obese cat. She died in a hospital. Her obesity had
a thousand health problems crash into her all at
once. She was nine when she died. It made me
believe that cats really do have nine lives. That's
when I learned to cry. I cried because I was living
in the country while my baby Mini was living in
the city with my father. I wasn't there to take

care of her like a mother should. I wasn't even able to give her a proper goodbye. Them vet nurses probably threw her in the garbage which hurts the most.

Sasha was poisoned and that's how she died. She died stumbling into the dark basement to die peaceful but completely alone.

I wish I was there for her but for some reason Allah (swt) didn't want me to and I trust him completely. I also want to thank him for teaching me that life on this dunya is short lived and that we should do good so we will have infinite enjoyment in Jannah. He has taught me this through the deaths of my cats

He also taught me that the kindness that I give to both animals and people will give me deeds that will help me in the hereafter.

Even though the death of my cats are tragic, each and every death has taught me something new. They are the extraordinary signs that Allah (swt) has given me from time to time. Thank you Allah. Thank you Allah. And thank you Allah.

These are the deaths of my cats

Allah (swt) and Me

I know the sins that I've committed
But I want to confess them
Even though you already know
Because you all are All-Knowing and the All-
Seeing
But repenting them to you makes me feel better
And that's what I'll do

You've already seen me repent to you but I feel
the need to draw out a picture
In the darkest of night
When everyone is asleep, but me
I crisscross my legs
And raise the palms of my hands to you
I speak softly, between a whisper and a firm
voice
While the tears stream down my face
With my hair in a mess
And my posture straight
I look at the palms of my hands, and I try to
focus on the lines that are carved into them
Trying to focus on these line through my tear-
filled eyes
As I focus on these lines, the thoughts of my sins
are flooding in my mind and squirting out of my
mouth.
My words full of regret and sorrow at the sins

but filled with hope that You, the All Merciful and All-Kind, will forgive me for all the sins I've done
I crave your attention because I know that you are the only one that truly listens to words that pour out of my mouth like a waterfall pouring off the edge of a cliff

I start with the recent sins which are fresh in my mind and my mouth travels back in time to the sins that haven't been left behind by my forgetfulness
When this happens, my heart seems to uplift from the heavy burden that it's been carrying for quite some time
The feeling of guiltiness drifts away and peace enters my heart in miniature tidal waves
That's when I feel the gentleness of Your mercy and see the beauty of Your kindness
Sin either great or little still affects me in so many an enormous ways, that you the All-Intelligent gave me the Quran to deal with my moods and pains
The Quran and duas have protected me in incredible ways

My sins vary from big to small, but in order to be a believer you have to realize you are a sinner too
Allah (swt) made people perfectly imperfect so we can see the power he has over us
He gave us the knowledge to understand our mistakes, to see the power in overcoming bad habits, and the beauty of implementing good ones

Asking the All-Forgiving for forgiveness is my
good habit to you
And it's a keeper for this dunya and in the
Hereafter too

I am human and I make mistakes
It's a part of my life
It's a part of ours too
And sometimes those mistakes shatter our souls
But everyone should remember that anything
that breaks can be fixed
Allah (swt) is the only one that can truly fix us
He can put us back together, piece by piece, flesh
and bone, till we're whole
And that is the undeniable truth

So when I repent, Allah makes me feel whole

And that is how my relationship with Allah (swt)
goes:
I break, He fixes,
I learn, He teaches,
I grow, He sees,
I misunderstand, He understands,

I'm alone, He's here for me
I'm scared, He comforts me
I'm confused, He informs me
I cry, He hears me
I love Him and He loves me

And I am glad to be the slave of the All-
Magnificent and All-Wise King!

Thank you Allah for blessing me in this dunya and I pray to see you in the Hereafter.

Insha allah

Beautiful Cousin

Beautiful Cousin, you are important to me
Being without you is a nightmare
Being with you is like a sweet dream that came
true

Beautiful Cousin, you are important to me
Your loyalty is sealed and permanently in my
heart
And your creativity manifest my mind

Beautiful Cousin, you are important to me
Cousins by chance and Sisters by choice
Your affection warms me endearingly

Beautiful Cousin, you are important to me
Your boldness strikes me in awe and your loving
arms comfort me
You are such a rarity that I'm blessed to see every
single day

Beautiful Cousin, you are important to me
Supportive in the best ways and your artistic side
moves me
You've helped me immensely

Beautiful Cousin, you are important to me
Your abundance of energy infects me

Your inspiration energizes me

Beautiful Cousin, you are important to me
Your fixation on fixing the little things humors
me
But the memories that we share will always be
inside of me

Beautiful Cousin, you are important to me
I have been blessed by Allah (swt) for sending
you my way since we were babies
And that our friendship will last infinitely

Beautiful Cousin, you are important to me
You lift me up when no one knows I've fallen
down
And that's the most beautiful thing of all

Beautiful Cousin, you are important to me
You understanding me amazingly important to
me
And me understanding you ignites me

Oh Beautiful Cousin, stay as you are.
Allah (swt) made you beautiful just the way you
are
And that's the most beautiful thing of all

This Question

This Question that everyone asks me,
Is tearing me apart like ripping a sheet of paper
in two.
No one knows the struggle of answering this
question, except me.
Everyone thinks this question is harmless, but
that's not true
Choosing. Picking. Deciding.
You're basically asking me if I love my hands or
my feet.
When you're missing the point, that I need both
to move

This Question that everyone asks me,
Instantly kills my mood
Why did that question have to escape your lips
for me to answer?
Why did your lips even have to move?
To asks this question in the middle of our
conversation, and I'm just like "What's your
problem dude?"

This Question that everyone asks me.
You only care about the answer because
somehow my answer will define my loyalty to
either place.
But I'm not going to pick a side

Because I am a mixture of both places
And to choose would be a lie

This Question that everyone asks me.
No one is ever satisfied when I don't pick a side
And that's fine
Because my answer of being neutral was never
meant to satisfy you
And that's definitely not a lie

This Question that everyone asks me.
Picking a side would be like taking a picture of
half of my body
Because you need the other side to complete the
puzzle of mine

This Question that everyone asks me.
Choosing would be like asking if I like my left or
right eye
But you're missing the big picture
I need both eyes to see
And I need them both to survive

This Question that everyone asks me is:
"Do you like to live in the City of Oakland or in
the Town of Robbins?"

The problem is that both places are a part of my
being and without the other place I'm not exactly
at peace and I'm most definitely torn
Born and raised in Oakland half my life and at
the moment being raised and growing in
Robbins
Oakland and Robbins are a package deal to me

I'm not separating the two because both places
have helped mold the woman that I am today

So I am forgiving everyone for asking me this
question. I know you never intended to make me
feel this way because of such a simple but yet,
complicated question that can have such an
effect on me

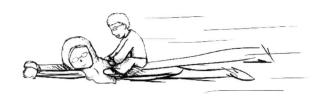

My Elias

My Elias
He is the definition of loyalty
To Family to Sport Teams

My Elias
He is the funniest guy I know
He will make you laugh till your eyes are filled
with tears

My Elias
Sweet as sugar
Complements come out of his mouth smoothly

My Elias
The loudest thing on the planet
He literally rocks your world

My Elias
Annoying little thing
He's your living alarm clock and reminder of all
events

My Elias
Love Bug
He'll hug you till you fall to the ground

My Elias

Tech Savvy
He knows techie language

My Elias
Strong Boy
He'll knock you down accidentally

My Elias
An Actor
He deserves the Best at Being Dramatic Award

My Elias
Kind-Hearted
He loves helping others out
My Elias
Good Big Brother
Always helping out with baby Maya

My Elias
Super Smart
Only when he wants to be

My Elias
Special Boy
For a special sister like Me

My Elias
Rare Being
You won't find anyone like him

My Elias
Sharp Man
Likes to keep his hair cut clean

My Elias
Muslim Man
He'll put that song on replay and he prays five
times a day in worship to Allah (swt)

My Elias
Really Friendly
Everyone loves him

My Elias
Baby Magnet
All the Babies love him

My Elias
A Real Flirty Boy
All the girls love him

My Elias
My Blessing
I am Blessed to be able to call him my brother
And I am so proud to be his older sister
I love you so much Elias and may Allah (swt)
guide you all the way to Jannah!

Conditioning a Yemeni

She observes her Mama silently as she's cleaning
the bathroom thoroughly.
She's mentally taking note of how her Mama
scrubs the tub smoothly but firmly and how she
wipes the bathroom mirror swiftly and carefully.
The bathroom seems to sparkle after her Mama
is done cleaning it.
Mama explains to her Daughter that in order to
be a Mara, a woman, she must clean her parents'
palace with perfection or no one will come for
her.
The Daughter nods her head and her Mama
smiles at her obedient princess.
The Daughter is only 12, her training has just
begun

He observes his Baba carefully as he's stacking
the different types of chips and candies in their
rightful places
He's mentally taking note of how his Baba puts
the gummy bears on the side shelf while he puts
the Hot Cheetos on the middle shelf.
The liquor store seems to smile after his Baba
was done organizing it.
Baba explains to his Son that in order to be a
Rajal, a man, he must organize his money with
precision or he'll never have a palace of his own

over his head
The Son nods his head and his Baba gives an
approving nod at his obedient heir to the throne
The Son is only 12, his conditioning has just
begun

She is being crushed by the stress of her parents'
needs and her responsibilities
She has mastered everything a Mara has to do
She knows how to clean the house with
perfection; she cooks the most exotic foods, both
American and Yemeni. She even knows how to
make Indian food too. She takes care of her little
siblings with ease and has maintained a 4.0 GPA
all the way through.
She doesn't know how long she can remain in
this prison like palace
Free time for herself has become a distant
memory.
But opportunity is waiting for her at high school
and college
The Daughter is 15 and she's waiting to break
free

He is being manipulated by the power of his
Baba's money and authority
He had excelled everything a Rajal has to do
He knows how to organize the cigarettes and
liquors with skill. He can make the customers
happy instantly with his great personality. He
even has many nicknames from his favorite
customers too
He has maintained some good grades, and he
has a new baby sister at home

He doesn't know how long he can be trapped in this cage-like liquor store anymore
Sleep has become a distant dream that he only gets infrequently
But freedom and fun are waiting behind those majestic doors of high school and college
The Son is 15 and he's waiting to fight his way out of this misery

School is a whole different story in the Yemeni community

There are two types of Yemeni kids at school. There are Yemeni girls and boys who are fighting for a better life. They're not going to start drama and are staying focused on the now and the future. They are thinking with their heads. Their friends are usually intelligent and kind people who help them think outside the box. Their favorite objects are books that have touched hearts in such a special way. Their favorite activity is meeting new people especially Muslim Yemenis who have upped their A game.

They are the ones who are rebellious for change

Then there are other Yemenis that have given up from the start. Lost hope the moment they learned to understand what's up. They know they are trapped and it's either that they have accepted it as fact or they lost hope in change. The girls wear take their disguises off once they set foot on school grounds. This is how they make present their true colors. Language instantly becomes crude when Yemenis are with their friends. They are contained at home but at school, freedom rings. Drugs stolen from the Baba's store. Make up kits taken from their Mama's rooms. Hormonal teens break loose at school. These kids have given up on change but they want to "live it up" before it's too late.

The Daughter and The Son are still trying to figure out who they are and who they want to be. But they're trying to understand this world through Yemeni American eyes. Through a Muslim point of view. They don't know if they fit in either Yemeni kid category. They just want to have peace and have an amazing life.

This is the life cycle of the Yemeni society.

About the Author

Noel Hassan is a 17-year-old Yemeni-American teenage girl, born in Oakland, California. Her lived experience is a cornucopia of histories, cultures and traditions. Hers is an important voice which gives us all a window to peer through to witness an essential narrative that has defined the early part of the 21st century. At the age of eight, her family relocated from Oakland to a quiet, rural country town named Robbins in Central California, instantly transporting her from the socially conscious, politically diverse surroundings of the Bay Area to a place that is socially and politically conservative with a population of about 300 people. It was here that the foundation of her home life began to change culminating in her finding her strength and the voice within.

One of four Muslim girls in elementary, middle and high school, writing became Noel's outlet for expression. School and her journal became the place where she would evolve from a girl to a young woman. Noel, at times, might be described as shy or a nerdy bookworm, but all of that changes with a pen in her hand; it is in that space where she musters the courage to write her deepest thoughts in poetic form to speak to the world one poem at a time. Noel writes to chronicle her journey through life and to connect with all who are open and willing to listen. May her poems enliven your heart, stimulate your mind, and bring nourishment to your soul.

Made in the USA
Columbia, SC
27 February 2020

88440059R00062